Isaiah 26:3-4
"PERFECT PEACE VI"

Isaiah 26:3-4
"PERFECT PEACE VI"
Zacchaeus

Vanessa Rayner

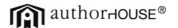 authorHOUSE®

AuthorHouse™ LLC
1663 Liberty Drive
Bloomington, IN 47403
www.authorhouse.com
Phone: 1-800-839-8640

The Scriptures' quotations are taken from the KJV, NIV and NLT.

The King James Version present on the Bible Gateway matches the 1987 printing. The KJV is public domain in the United States.

The Holy Bible, New International Version, NIV Copyright© 1973, 1978, 1984, 2011 by Biblica, Inc. Used by permission. All rights reserved worldwide.

Scripture quotations marked (NLT) are taken from the Holy Bible, New Living Translation, copyright c 1996, 2004, 2007 by Tyndale House Foundation. Used by permission of Tyndale House Publishers, Inc., Carol Stream, Illinois 60188. All rights reserved.

Published by AuthorHouse   02/25/2014

ISBN: 978-1-4918-6792-1 (sc)
ISBN: 978-1-4918-6791-4 (e)

Any people depicted in stock imagery provided by Thinkstock are models, and such images are being used for illustrative purposes only. Certain stock imagery © Thinkstock.

This book is printed on acid-free paper.

Because of the dynamic nature of the Internet, any web addresses or links contained in this book may have changed since publication and may no longer be valid. The views expressed in this work are solely those of the author and do not necessarily reflect the views of the publisher, and the publisher hereby disclaims any responsibility for them.

A GIFT . . .

*P*resented to

_____

*F*rom

_____

*D*ate

_____

Many books can Inform You;
Only one can Transform You!

CONTENTS

THEME

Thou wilt keep him in perfect peace, whose mind is stayed on thee: because he trusteth in thee. Trust ye in the LORD for ever: for in the LORD JEHOVAH is everlasting strength. Isaiah 26:3-4 KJV

You will keep in perfect peace those whose minds are steadfast, because they trust in you. Trust in the LORD forever, for the LORD, the LORD himself, is the rock eternal. Isaiah 26:3-4 NIV

You will keep in perfect peace all who trust in you, all whose thoughts are fixed on you! Trust in the LORD always, for the LORD GOD is the eternal Rock. Isaiah 26:3-4 NLT

Question: Which of the above verses are considered a paraphrase version of the Bible.

Answer: In the 2nd book title, <u>Isaiah 26:3-4</u> "<u>The Last Single Digit</u>," chapter 1.

Smile . . . .

PRAYER

Father God, I pray that this book will
inspire and bless your people.
Enable them to keep their minds
on YOU, even the more.

Father God, I thank You for blessing
those that help make
Your Work and Word go forth.

Father, your words, promise to reward
those that bless your servant.
It could be by prayer, words of encouragement,
to even given that person a cup of water.

**Anyone who welcomes you welcomes me,
And anyone who welcomes me
welcomes the one who sent me.
And if anyone gives even a cup of cold water
to one of these little ones who is my disciple,
Truly I tell you that person will
certainly not lose their reward.**
Matthew 10:40, 42 NIV

In Jesus' Name, I Pray, Amen.

AUTHOR'S NOTES

Author notes normally provide a way to add extra information to one's book that may be awkward and inappropriate to include in the text of the book itself. It provides supplemental contextual details on the aspects of the book. It can help readers understand the book content and the background details of the book better. The times and dates of researching, reading, and gathering this information are not included; mostly when I typed on it.

0633; Sunday, January 6, 2013; I had a dream about sitting in a tall tree. I was sitting comfortably on a thick brownish branch. I was excited, anxious and my heart was beating fast with joy. When I woke up, Zacchaeus was on my mind.

NOTE: I need to read over Perfect Peace IV and finish writing Perfect Peace V; but I'm going forth with Perfect Peace VI title <u>Zacchaeus</u> in Jesus' name. Amen.

0505; Monday, January 7, 2013

0702; Tuesday, January 8, 2013

Vanessa Rayner

0538; Wednesday, January 9, 2013

2132; Thursday, September 5, 2013. Just realized I was working on book VII in the series.

0526; Friday, September 6, 2013. Dad's Birthday; Mom's Homegoing Celebration Day. PS: Don't forget to check out the book I dedicated to them, Isaiah 26:3-4 "Perfect Peace V" 2541.

0609; Monday, September 9, 2013

0500; Wednesday, September 11, 2013

0428; Thursday, September 12, 2013

0840; Sunday, September 22, 2013

0754; Thursday, September 26, 2013

2110; Friday, September 27, 2013

0653; Saturday, September 28, 2013

0858; Monday, September 30, 2013

1151; Tuesday, October 1, 2013

0735; Wednesday, October 2, 2013

0709; Thursday, October 3, 2013

Isaiah 26:3-4 "Perfect Peace VI"

0741; Saturday, October 5, 2013

1121; Sunday, October 6, 2013

1914; Monday, October 7, 2013. 1st day on the new job "O'Reilly Auto Parts"

0747; Saturday, October 12, 2013

1856; Sunday, October 13, 2013

1718; Monday, October 14, 2013

0136; Friday, October 18, 2013

0700; Saturday, October 19, 2013

0927; Sunday, October 20, 2013

0921; Thursday, October 24, 2013

0646; Tuesday, October 29, 2013

0708; Saturday, November 2, 2013; Trying to work on this book, but my mind is constantly thinking about "Strongholds." I have been up early this morning praying for "Hus-bee" and myself. I know God is able, but . . . YOU got to be willing . . .

0630; Sunday, November 3, 2013

0420; Tuesday, November 5, 2013

Vanessa Rayner

0535; Thursday, November 7, 2013

0715; Friday, November 8, 2013; I'm gonna work on Father' book before I go to O'Reilly Auto Parts; it been 1 month and 1 day. Hallelujah is the highest Praise!

0741; Monday, November 11, 2013

0415; Tuesday, November 12, 2013

2234; Monday, November 18, 2013

0001; Tuesday, November 19, 2013

1603; Saturday, November 23, 2013

0530; Monday, December 2, 2013

0613; Tuesday, December 3, 2013

0450; Wednesday, December 4, 2013

0538; Thursday, December 5, 2013

0616; Friday, December 6, 2013

0638; Tuesday, December 10, 2013

0722; Saturday, December 14, 2013

0624; Monday, December 16, 2013

0715; Saturday, December 21, 2013

1945; Tuesday, December 24, 2013

1811; Sunday, December 29, 2013

0656; Thursday, January 9, 2014

1727; Tuesday, January 14, 2014

1928; Friday, January 17, 2014; Just me and you Lord, again!!!

1858; Wednesday, January 22, 2014

2013; Friday, January 24, 2014

0920; Saturday, January 25, 2014

1020; Tuesday, January 28, 2014

1823; Wednesday, January 30, 2014

0729; Friday, January 31, 2014; Proofreading & working on book VII. Off three days in a row from O'Reilly Auto Parts. I like my job "Father God," *Hub Delivery Driver.* A little more $$$ would be nice, Father, if you ask me. LOL with Father God.

1619; Saturday, February 1, 20014

0114; Sunday, February 2, 2014

0925; Saturday, February 15, 2014; Looking over Zacchaeus one more time before I sent it to AuthorHouse, Glory be to God!

0457; Sunday, February 16, 2014; Sent manuscript to AuthorHouse

PREFACE

Isaiah 26:3-4, "Perfect Peace VI"
~ Zacchaeus

This book is the 6th book of a series of Isaiah 26:3-4, "Perfect Peace" collection. It all started from how I drew near to the LORD in my workplace by keeping my mind on Him. I related numbers; you see throughout the day, everywhere, on almost everything on Him, His word, biblical events and facts.

My desire is for you to discover the power of the Holy Spirit concerning the biblical event recorded in Luke 19:1-10.

Remember, the LORD Jesus <u>PROMISED us tribulation</u> while we were in this world.

*These things, I have spoken unto you,
that in me ye might have peace.
In the world ye shall have tribulation:
But be of good cheer; I have
overcome the world.*
John 16:33 KJV

However, we have been <u>PROMISED His peace</u> while we endure these short trials, tribulations, troubles, and tests. Perfect Peace is given only to those whose mind and heart reclines upon the LORD. God's peace is increased in us according to the knowledge the LORD gives to us from His Word.

> ***Grace and peace be multiplied unto you***
> ***through the knowledge of God,***
> ***and of Jesus our LORD.***
> 2 Peter 1:2 KJV

THANKS

First, I'd like to say, as a disciple of the LORD, we can rest assure that when we are seeking His plan and purpose for our lives, we will be successful, because true success lies in doing God's will; not in fame and fortune.

Be Encourage . . . Thanks for your support.

ACKNOWLEDGEMENT

I would like to express my gratitude to **ALL** of God's people. Thanks & Remember, "The GIFTS are still in YOU!"

**For the gifts and calling of God
are without repentance.**
Romans 11:29 KJV
(Official Authorized Version, 1611)

It attempts to keep the exact words & phrases
of the original manuscript.

For God's gifts and his call are irrevocable.
Romans 11:29 NIV
(Thought for thought translation of the Bible, 1978)

**For God's gifts and his call can
never be withdrawn.**
Romans 11:29 NLT
(Paraphrase Version of the Bible; 1996)

INTRODUCTION

I woke up from a dream this morning about 6:33 am. I remember, I was in a tall tree, sitting comfortably on a thick brownish branch. I was happy, anxious, exciting, and my heart was beating very fast with joy. I really didn't know why. I was just excited! Soon after I prayed about it, Zacchaeus came to my mind. Quite frankly, at this moment about 8:45 am on January 6, 2013, I'm not sure what I will be relating Zacchaeus, and Luke 19:1-10 to in the bible.

You know; the LORD can't hold you responsible for a dream if you don't understand it. The LORD will answer dreams He gives you if you ask.

"Ask and it will be given to you;
seek and you will find;
knock and the door will be opened to you.
For everyone who asks receives;
the one who seeks finds;
and to the one who knocks,
the door will be opened.
Matthew 7:7-8 NIV

Be enlightened, and enjoy the peace it will bring in Jesus' Name. Amen.

NOTE: I need to read over Perfect Peace IV and finish writing Perfect Peace V, but I'm going forth with Perfect Peace VI title <u>Zacchaeus</u> in Jesus' name. Amen.

DEDICATION

I would like to dedicate this book to all the
"Z A C C H A E U S" in the world.

CHAPTER 1

Gospel of Luke

The Gospel of Luke is the 3rd and longest of the four gospels. It was written around 62 BC. The Gospel of Luke in the King James Bible has 24 chapters, 1,151 verses and about 25,939 words. The earliest manuscripts were given the title "Gospel According to Luke." The word "gospel" means "good news." Now, the "Gospel of Luke" is simply called "Luke."

The Gospel of Luke was written by Luke the physician, a man of attentions and details. It is a detailed account of Jesus of Nazareth's birth, life, ministry, death, resurrection and ascension. It is known as a Synoptic Gospel because it includes many of the same biblical events, often in the same sequence, and sometimes in the same wording as Matthew and Mark. The term synoptic comes from the Greek "syn" meaning "together" and "optic" meaning "seen."

The understanding is that the Gospel of Mark was the first of the synoptic gospels and that it served as a source for Matthew and Luke's Gospel. The Gospel of Mark was written around the destruction of the Temple of Jerusalem, around 70 AD. Mark's gospel is quite short. It has only 16 chapters and is written in Koine Greek. The Synoptic Gospels are the primary source of historical information about Jesus.

Note of Interest: What other two languages was the Bible originally written in? *Answer in back of book.*

All three writers attest that Jesus Christ is the Son of God, but the Gospel of Luke emphases the humanity of Jesus. It shows Jesus' compassion for the weak, the suffering and the outcast. Luke's gospel account also places a special importance on the activities of the Holy Spirit. In fact, the Gospel of Luke speaks of the Holy Spirit more than Matthew or Mark; the other two synoptic gospels.

John the Baptist is filled with the Holy Spirit even before he is born. John's mother Elizabeth is filled with the Holy Spirit, and before long, John's speechless father Zachariah is also filled with the Holy Spirit.

The Holy Spirit revealed to Simeon, a righteous and devout man in Jerusalem that he would see the Messiah before he dies, Luke 2:26-27. John the Baptist announces that one who is more powerful than him was coming after him and will baptize with the Holy Spirit and with fire, Luke 3:16.

When Jesus was baptized by John the Baptist, the Holy Spirit descended on Him in bodily form like a dove, and God the Father confirms from heaven that Jesus is His beloved Son, Luke 3:22. Shortly after, Jesus being filled with the Holy Spirit is led by the Spirit into the wilderness, where the devil tempted Him for forty days, Luke 4:1-2. Having successfully resisted the devil, Luke 4:4, 8, 12, Jesus returns to Galilee in the power of the Holy Spirit, Luke 4:14.

The Gospel of Luke is the only gospel with a formal introduction, in which Luke, the writer explains his purpose. Luke states that he too wishes to write an orderly account for Theophilus, so that Theophilus "may know the certainty of the things been taught." It has been suggested that Luke's address to the "Most Excellent Theophilus," may be a reference to the Roman-imposed High Priest of Israel around that era who name was Theophilus ben Ananus. The name Theophilus means "friend of God" or "loved by God."

Luke's Gospel recounts a royal genealogy and a virgin birth for Jesus. Luke the Evangelist traces Jesus' lineage back to Adam, indicating a universal sense of salvation.

The Gospel of Luke is the only gospel which contains the angel Gabriel's Announcement of the Birth of Jesus to Mary, Luke 1:28-33. It has pertinent facts regarding the conception and birth of Jesus that are not brought to light in the other gospel accounts. It tells about the conception of Jesus, brought about by the Holy Spirit, Luke 1:35, and the song Mary sang after hearing the news, Luke 1:46-56. The Gospel of

Luke, also records the song Zechariah sung after the birth of his son, John the Baptist, Luke 1:67-79.

NOTE: Their songs are in the back of the book, for your convenience.

The Christmas story account of the birth of Jesus is taken from Luke's Gospel. In brief, the pregnant Mary with Joseph travels to Bethlehem for a census issued by Caesar Augustus, the Roman Emperor. Joseph and Mary had to travel to their ancestral towns to register for this census. While they were there, she gave birth. She wrapped him in strips of cloth and laid him in a manger because there were no rooms available for them in the inn. That night, some shepherds were in the fields nearby watching their sheep. An angel of the Lord told the shepherds that today your Savior was born in the town of David. He is the Christ, the Lord. The shepherds hurried to Bethlehem to worship Him, Luke 2.

The Gospel of Luke records the circumcision of Jesus on the eighth day, and the mother's purification rites in accordance with the Law of Moses, Luke 2. The only incident about Jesus' childhood, at the age of 12 is recorded in the book of Luke as Jesus remains behind in the Temple of Jerusalem after the Feast of Passover. There, he was listening and asking questions with the religious teachers of the law, and they were astonished, Luke 2. Luke records Jesus first words spoken to his parents indicating His divine sonship to God, the father:

**"And He said unto them, How
is it that ye sought me?
Wist ye not that I must be about
my Father's business?**
Luke 2:49 KJV

*Question: What is the Feast of the Passover? Answer in
back of book.*

Although first-century cultures usually minimized
the importance of women, Luke portrayed women
as significant in the early church. Luke shows how
women played an important role among Jesus'
followers. The Gospel of Luke devotes more attention
to women, more than the other gospels.

1. Elizabeth, the mother of John the Baptist, Luke 1

2. Mary, the mother of Jesus, Luke 2

3. The Prophetess Anna blessed the child Jesus,
    Luke 2:36-38

4. Simon Peter's mother-in-law was healed by
    Jesus, Luke 4:38-39

5. Widow of Nain son was raised from the dead by
    Jesus, Luke 7:11-15

6. A sinful woman anointed Jesus' feet at the
    Pharisees dinner, Luke 7:36-38

7. Women were part of Jesus' traveling party and helped support him out of their own means, provide, Luke 8:1-3

   1. Mary Magdalene who had been freed from seven demons

   2. Joanna, the wife of Chuza, the manager of Herod's household

   3. Susanna, and many others

8. Jairus' 12 year old daughter was healed by Jesus, Luke 8:41, 49-55

9. An anonymous woman was healed from a bleeding disorder by Jesus, Luke 8:43-49

10. Mary sat at the Lord's feet, and listened while Martha was distracted by the big dinner preparation, Luke 10:38-42

11. An anonymous woman in the crowd blesses Jesus' mother, Luke 11:27-28

12. A woman who had been crippled 18 years were healed by Jesus on the Sabbath day, Luke 13:10-13

13. A woman in a parable concerning leaven, Luke 13:20

14. A woman in a parable found a lost coin, Luke 15:8-10

15. A widow in a parable kept going to the judge to obtain justice, Luke 18:1-8

16. A poor widow gave two small coins to the temple, Luke 21:1-4

17. A servant girl states that Peter was one of Jesus' followers, which he denies, Luke 22:54-57

18. Grief-stricken women were among those who followed along, and observed the crucifixion, Luke 23:27, 49

19. Women prepared spices to anoint Jesus' body, Luke 23:55-56

20. Women were the first to find Jesus' tomb empty, Luke 24:1-6

21. Angels told women that Jesus had risen, Luke 24:6-8

22. Women were the first to tell the other disciples, Luke 24:9-11

    1. Mary Magdalene

    2. Joanna

    3. Mary the mother of James

The Gospel of Luke records Jesus reading the book of the prophet Isaiah in the synagogue:

**"The Spirit of the Lord is upon me,
because he has anointed me
to proclaim good news to the poor.
He has sent me to proclaim
freed for the prisoners
and recovery of sight for the blind,
to set the oppressed free,
to proclaim the year of the Lord's favour."**
Luke 4:18-19 NIV

Then Jesus closed the book, and gave it back to the attendant, sat down, and said the Scripture you've just heard has been fulfilled this very day!

The Gospel of Luke emphasizes that Jesus had committed no crime against Rome as confirmed by Herod, Pilate, and the thief crucified with Jesus. Roman involvement in Jesus' execution is downplayed, and Luke's gospel places most of the responsibility on the Jews. In Luke's Passion narrative, Jesus prays that God forgive those who crucify him and his assurance to a crucified thief that they will be together in Paradise.

The Gospel of Luke tells the story of two disciples on the road to Emmaus. Jesus' commission to the disciples to carry his message to all the nations affirms Christianity as a universal religion.

The Gospels records a total of 37 miracles. The Gospel of Luke records 22 of those miracles, and 6 of those miracles were not recorded by the other writers. The following is a list of those miracles.

1. Miraculous draught of fishes, Luke 5:1-11

2. Young man from Nain, Luke 7:11-17

3. An infirm Woman, Luke 13:10-17

4. Man with dropsy, Luke 14:1-6

5. Cleansing ten lepers, Luke 17:11-19

6. Healing the ear of a servant, Luke 22:49-51

The other 16 are:

1. Exorcism at the Synagogue in Capernaum

2. Cleansing a Leper, Luke 5:12-16

3. The Centurion's Servant, Luke 7:1-10

4. Healing the Peter's mother in law, Luke 4:38-41

5. Exorcising at sunset, Luke 4:40-41

6. Calming the storm, Luke 8:22-25

7. Gerasenes demonic, Luke 8:26-39

8. Paralytic at Capernaum, Luke 5:17-26

9. Daughter of Jairus, Luke 8:40-56

10. Woman Healed from Chronic Bleeding, Luke 8:43-48

11. Man with the withered Hand, Luke 6:6-11

12. Exorcising the blind and mute man, Luke 11:14-23

13. Feeding the 5000 people, Luke 9:10-17

14. Transfiguration of Jesus, Luke 9:28-36

15. Boy possessed by a demon, Luke 9:37-49

16. Blind near Jericho, Luke 18:35-43

In the Gospel of Luke, there are 27 parables about the teaching of Jesus, and 14 of the 27 parables are only recorded in Luke's gospel. They are underlined.

1. New Wine in Old Wineskins, Luke 5:37-39

2. Wise and Foolish Builders, Luke 6:47-49

3. The Creditor and Two Debtors, Luke 7:41-43

4. The Sower, Luke 8:4-15

5. A Candle under a Bushel, Luke 8:16-18

6. The Good Samaritan, Luke 10:30-37

7. Friend in Need, Luke 11:5-13

8. The Strong Man, Luke 11:21-22

9. The Rich Fool, Luke 12:15-21

10. The Faithful Servant, Luke 12:35-48

11. The Barren Fig Tree, Luke 13:6-9

12. The Mustard Seed, Luke 13:18-19

13. The Leaven, Luke 13:20-21

14. The Wedding Feast, Luke 14:7-14

15. The Great Banquet, Luke 14:15-24

16. Counting the Cost, Luke 14:25-35

17. The Lost Sheep, Luke 15:1-7

18. The Lost Coin, Luke 15:8-10

19. The Prodigal Son, Luke 15:11-32

20. The Unjust Steward, Luke 16:1-13

21. The Rich Man and Lazarus, Luke 16:19-31

22. The Master and Servant, Luke 17:7-10

23. Persistent Widow, Luke 18:1-8

24. The Pharisee and the Tax Collector, Luke 18:9-14

25. The Ten Minas, Luke 19:11-27

26. The Wicked Husbandmen, Luke 20:9-19

27. The Fig Tree, Luke 21:29-33

It is also Luke who uniquely records the calling of Zaccheaus in Jericho. There in the city, Jesus met Zaccheaus, a chief tax collector, working for the Romans, hated and despised by those he collected from, especially his own people.

CHAPTER 2

Luke the Evangelist

Luke, the Evangelist is one of the four evangelists who wrote the "Gospel of Jesus Christ." The early church fathers credit him as the author of the "Gospel according to Luke" and the "Acts of the Apostles." The early tradition witnessed by the Muratorian Canon, Irenaeus, Clement of Alexandria, Origen, and Tetullian, held that the Gospel of Luke and Acts of the Apostles were both written by Luke, a companion of Paul. Luke doesn't mention his own name in these books. It was later reaffirmed by prominent figures in early Christianity, Jerome and Eusebius that Luke is the author of these two books.

* *

The 4-1-1 *(Lil Info)* on Muratorian Canon, Irenaeus, Clement of Alexandria, Origen, Tetullian, Jerome and Eusebius in back of book.

* *

The name Luke is a Greek name and means illuminate, to enlighten, to shed light on an item or subject. Luke the Evangelist was of Greek origin born in the Hellenistic city of Antioch in Ancient Syria, and one of the early converts from paganism. Little is known about Luke's parents or whether or not he had sisters or brothers. What is known is that Luke's parents were not of the Hebrew race, and Luke was unmarried and didn't have any children. Luke was a Gentile, the only Gentile writer in New Testament, and the first Christian Doctor.

In Apostle Paul's final greeting to the Colossians, he makes a clear distinction between Luke, the gentile, and those "who are of the circumcision," a term which refers to Jews, Colossians 4.

**Aristarchus my fellowprisoner saluteth you,
and Marcus, sister's son of Barnabas,
(touching whom ye received commandments:
if he come unto you, receive him;)
and Jesus, which is called Justus,
who are of the circumcision.
These only are my fellowworkers
unto the kingdom of God,
which have been a comfort unto me.
Epaphras, who is one of you, a
servant of Christ, saluteth you,
always laboring fervently for you in
prayers that ye may stand perfect
and complete in all the will of God.
For I bear him record, that he
hath a great zeal for you,
and them that are in Laodicea,
and them in Hierapolis.**

**Luke, the beloved physician,
and Demas, greet you.
Salute the brethren which are in
Laodicea, and Nymphas,
and the church which is in his house.**
Colossians 4:10-15 KJV

Just an Interesting Note: The verse, "Salute the brethren which are in Laodicea, and Nymphas, and the church which is in **his** house" states "Salute the brethren which are in Laodicea and Nymphas and the church which is in **her** house" in the following version of the bible: Amplified, CEB, CEV, ESV, Message, NASB, NIV, NLT. In fact, Nymphas is a name that is given to a woman. I must say, Phoebe is recognized as the first woman deacon mentioned in Romans 16:1-2 in the Christian church in Cenchreae.

Luke was a man of integrity and intelligence. He was extremely educated and a physician by trade. His studies included Greek philosophy, medicine, and art in his youth. The writers of the ancient Church inform us that Luke was the first to paint the image of the All-Holy Theotokos, holding in her arms the pre-eternal Infant, our Lord Jesus Christ. Later, he painted two other icons of the All-Holy Theotokos. When they were brought before the Mother of God for her approval, she said, "May the grace of Him Who was born of me and my mercy be with these icons!" Luke also painted the distinguish images of the Apostles Peter and Paul.

It is not sure when Luke became a Christian, but he becomes a disciple of the Apostle Paul and later follows Paul until his martyrdom. He serves the Lord continuously filled with the Holy Spirit.

It is believed that Luke himself did not meet Jesus in the flesh, and was not an eye-witness of the ministry of Jesus according to Luke 1:1-4. It is viewed that Luke wrote his gospel after gathering the best sources of information within his reach. It is believed that Luke used the Gospel of Mark as one of his sources. The detailed information about Jesus' infancy was probably told to him by Mary, Jesus' mother. The unique material in the Gospel of Luke is said to derive from material collected during Paul's imprisonment in Caesarea, when Luke attended to him. Luke also refers to the fact that he is intending to write more of a chronological account, and also to build on the work of others.

In the New Testament, Luke is mentioned three times. Apostle Paul is the only person that mentions Luke name. It is mentioned in Colossians 4, 2 Timothy 4, and Philemon 1. He is referred to as a physician in the Pauline epistle to the Colossians.

Luke, the beloved physician,
and Demas, greet you.
Colossians 4:14 KJV

Luke name is mentioned again by Paul in his final words to Timothy in 2nd Timothy 4, as being by his side. Paul was in imprisoned again under Emperor Nero 66-67 AD.

Only Luke is with me.
Take Mark, and bring him with thee:
for he is profitable to me for the ministry.
2 Timothy 4:11 KJV

Then finally Luke is mentioned in Paul's final greetings in the epistle to Philemon, which has only one chapter.

There salute thee Epaphras, my
fellowprisoner in Christ Jesus;
Marcus, Aristarchus, Demas,
Lucas, my fellowlabouers.
The grace of our Lord Jesus Christ
be with your spirit. Amen.
Philemon 1:23-25 KJV

Luke documents the beginning of Paul's second missionary journey at the end of Acts, chapter 15, after "The Jerusalem Council."

Note: The Jerusalem Council was a conference of the Christian Apostles in Jerusalem about 50 AD. They decreed that Gentile Christians did not have to observe the Jewish Mosaic Laws for the Jews. Still some of the Judaic Christians from Jerusalem wanted the Gentile Christians from Antioch in Syria to obey the Mosaic custom of circumcision. A delegation led by the Apostle

Paul and his companion Barnabas was appointed to compare views with the elders of the church in Jerusalem, Acts 15:1-35.

The Apostle Paul decided to begin another journey to encourage the churches that had been planted and revisit the cities that were evangelized on the first missionary journey by him and his companions. The journey was traveled on foot and by sea and took them to at least 16 cities and over approximately 2800 miles.

As the preparation and planning for the second journey began, there ensured a "sharp disagreement" Acts 15:36-41 among Paul and Barnabas. The conflict involved whether to bringing John Mark with them on the journey or to leave him behind. Barnabas wanted to take John Mark, but Paul believed it was unwise and, therefore, strongly opposed.

John Mark had traveled with them previously, on the first missionary journey but had abandoned them in Pamphylia. The argument was so great that the result was a division into two missionary teams. Instead of traveling with Barnabas, Paul took Silas and left for Asia Minor. Barnabas took John Mark and set sail for Cyprus. In the book of Acts, Luke describes the events of the journey of Paul rather than Barnabas.

Note of Interest: About the argument, the story of the disagreement between Paul and Barnabas does not make a pleasant reading. By Luke recording it helps us to remember that the two men as they said to the people of Lustra that they were human beings. It is true that the Bible describes real human beings not superheroes doing the work of God. In time, John Mark did redeem himself to Paul, he is later seen serving with Paul and Peter, Colossians 4:10, 2 Timothy 4:11, Philemon 1:23-24, 1 Peter 5:13. Praise God Saints!

Luke accompanied Apostle Paul on a vast portion of his 3rd missionary journey. When Luke returned from collecting alms in Corinth for the poor, he departs with the Apostle Paul for Palestine on his third missionary journey. In the summer of 53 AD, they start this journey by revisiting the churches in Galatia, visited brethren in the Phrygia province, Acts 18:23. In the Autumn 54 AD to early Winter 57 AD, they journey from the Phrygia region to Ephesus and Paul stayed in the city about 3 years, Acts 19:1-20.

When Apostle Paul was kept under guard in prison in the city of Caesarea, Luke remained by his side. Luke was still by Paul side when he was sent to Rome to stand trial before Caesar. Luke endured all the difficulties of their voyage across the sea with Paul and nearly lost his life, Acts, chapters 27-28.

In Rome is where Luke wrote his Gospel and Acts of the Apostles. The Apostle Paul was released after two years in a Roman prison. He departs Rome to visit churches he had founded, and Luke was his companion again.

Vanessa Rayner

Shortly after, the Emperor Nero initiated a cruel persecution against the Christians in Rome. The Apostle Paul returned to Rome to encourage the persecuted Church. He was arrested and imprisoned again. The Evangelist Luke still wouldn't forsake his teacher, during this period of time of distress.

Apostle Paul compared himself to a victim doomed to be slaughtered. He tells Timothy to do his best to come to him quickly. Paul let him know that Demas, Crescens, and Titus have gone; and only Luke is with him, 2 Timothy 4:6, 10-11.

After Evangelist Luke's teacher, Apostle Paul was executed; he travels to Italy, Dalmatia, Gaul, and Macedonia spreading the Gospel of Jesus Christ. The Evangelist Luke then makes a journey to Egypt in his old age. He converts many to Christ as he passes through Libya, and Thebaid of Egypt. In the city of Alexandria, Luke ordained a bishop named Abillius to be a successor to Annas. He had carried out his ministry for 22 years. After Evangelist Luke returns to Greece, he set up churches mainly in Boeotia. He ordained priests and deacons for these churches. While he was there, he also healed those who were sick.

It is unclear about the death of Luke, whether he died by natural causes or martyr's death at the age of 84 in Achaia. Luke may have met his demises at the hands of idolatrous Greek priests in Boeotia, who crucified him on an olive tree in lieu of a cross, and his precious body was buried in Thebes, the principal city of Boeotia where Luke's holy relics were responsible for a multitude of healings.

However, other say that Luke died in Thebes, and the secretion from his holy body healed those suffering from eye diseases. The miracles of healing at his grave site continued for many years, and people came from near and far came for healing.

The location of the relics of St. Luke became known in 4 AD because of the healings that were occurring there. When the persecution of Christians came to a halt, the relics of Luke were transported to Constantinople by the orders of Constantius, son of Constantine the Great in 357 AD.

During the transfer of the holy relics of St. Luke to the church, a miracle occurred. A certain eunuch was afflicted with an incurable illness. He had spent a great a lot of money on physicians, and yet he wasn't cured. When he approached the holy and precious relics of the St. Luke with faith, he was healed, immediately. The relics of St. Luke were buried beneath the altar with the relics of the holy Apostles Andrew and Timothy. There they were reverence by the Orthodox Christians.

CHAPTER 3

The Chief Tax Collector

~ Luke 19:1-10

Over 2,000 years ago, when Jesus entered Jericho and was passing through, a man was there by the name of Zacchaeus. He was a chief tax collector and was extremely wealthy. He wanted to see who Jesus was, but because he was a short man, he could not see over the crowd. So he ran ahead, and climbed a sycamore-fig tree to see him, since Jesus was coming that way, that day.

When Jesus reached the spot where Zacchaeus was over him, up in the tree, he looked up and said to him, "Zacchaeus, come down immediately. I must stay at your house today." So he came down at once and welcomed him gladly. All the people saw this and began to mutter, "He has gone to be the guest of a sinner."

In spite of the crowd's muttering complains, Zacchaeus stood up and said to the Jesus, "Look, Lord! Here and now, I give half of my possessions to the poor, and if I have cheated anybody out of anything, I will pay back four times the amount." Jesus said to him, "Today salvation has come to this house, because this man, too, is a son of Abraham.

For the Son of Man came to seek, and to save the lost."

You Know?

Back then, when the Bible was written, a person's name was to reveal his or her destiny, character or personality. In Hebrew, the name that Zacchaeus' parents named him means "righteous one," "pure." It's likely that Zacchaeus' parents were Jewish who lived in the area of Jericho. They were worshippers of the God of Israel, and they had raised Zacchaeus in this manner. His destiny was to carry on his family's religious beliefs, to walk in the ways of the Lord and truly be "righteous," but he had apparently gone astray. Instead, he was hated by all the Pharisees and scribes in the area. Zacchaeus was defying his family's wishes, and he was going against God's plan for his life.

Most of the time, when the Bible mentions a publican, or a tax collect it is referring to a regular tax collector rather than a chief tax collector. According to chapter 19 of the Gospel of Luke, Zacchaeus was a chief tax collector at Jericho. This is the only time the title "chief" is used with the words "tax collector." This means that he was the head of the local taxation office, responsible to the Roman authorities for employment and management of the local tax collectors, and their moneys. Zacchaeus is not mentioned in the other gospels.

According to the above passage of scripture, Zacchaeus was a short man, lacking in height, but very wealth. However, at this particular time, when he met Jesus he was lacking in spiritually. When we are out of God's will for our lives, there is a spiritual battle being fought inside of us, and we are being cut down from what our spiritual size could really be.

God has directed us to walk down the path of righteousness. When we chose another path, we become torn apart on the inside. When we are out of God's will for our lives we, feel very small in spirit. And let's remember, we all have sinned and fall short.

For all have sinned, and come
short of the glory of God;
Romans 3:23 KJV

Zacchaeus likely felt what many of us felt when we were out of fellowship with God. When we are out of God's will, we can experience and feel depressed, destitute, and become immoral self-indulgent. Zacchaeus may have been spiritual short on the inside, but as Jesus of Nazareth was about to pass that way, he had a desire just to look upon the Savior. He had probably heard that this rabbi was different and knew he had the reputation of being friends with publicans and sinners. He had probably heard that even one of his own disciples was a former tax collector.

Who was that person? *Answer in back of the book, just in case it slipped your mind . . . smile*

It's as though he found a desire for a new life, for we read, "So he ran ahead and climbed a sycamore-fig tree to see him since Jesus was coming that way." In that time, it was unusual for a man to run, especially a wealth top Roman tax official. Nevertheless, in spite of, Zacchaeus ran probably as fast as he possibly could, down that dusty road that day. I can just imagine Zacchaeus an old heavy-set man, clothed in distinguished clothes with elaborate accessories, for the crowd recognized him. There was something about a man named "Jesus" that made Zacchaeus want to see him no matter what he had to do.

Zacchaeus could have been hindered from seeing Jesus by excuses. In the passage of scripture, we find out that a large crowd of people were there who were much taller than him, and was blocking his view. He probably could have complained about a number of things. However, he didn't offer up any excuses for his physical size, the people, dusty road, a need to climb a tree, and who might see him in the tree. Zacchaeus thought about how he could see Jesus, and muster up the strength to rise above the crowd of people in order to look upon the Savior.

People that sincerely desire to see Jesus will break down barriers, kick in doors, climb the highest mountain, walk through the valley of death, and be willing to go alone. When we truly have the desire to see Jesus we will find Him.

**I love those who love me, and
those who seek me find me.**
Proverbs 8:17 NIV

**You will seek me and find me when
you seek me with all your heart.**
Jeremiah 29:13 NIV

It appears to me, Jesus of Nazareth was not at all surprised that Zacchaeus was in the sycamore-fig tree. According to verses 5 and 6, "When Jesus came to the place, He looked up, and saw him, and said unto him, Zacchaeus, make haste, and come down; for today I must abide at thy house. And he made haste, and came down, and received him joyfully." I know this was the most joyfully day of Zacchaeus' life, and he will never be the same. *Praise God, Saint!*

Joy is one of the key themes in Luke's gospel. It is found 11 times in Luke's gospel, more than the other three gospels, (Matthew 6, Mark 0 and John 7). Joy is a quality with Jesus, and not just an emotion. It's based upon Jesus Christ whom it comes from. Joy remains with us through tribulations, trials and testing that will occur in our lives. It's far better to experience "joy in our soul" than "happiness." Happiness is something that occurs when things in life are happening the way we want, but joy is not based on happenings.

In those verses, we see that Jesus addressed Zacchaeus by name and told him to come down, and invited Himself into Zacchaeus' house. The crowd was shocked that Jesus, a Jew would defile himself by being a guest of a tax collector; but Zacchaeus received him joyfully. Zacchaeus publicly repented of corrupt acts, and vowed to make restitution for them, and held a feast at his house.

Notice in verses 7-10, "The crowd complained that Zacchaeus, the tax collector was a sinner." They had put him with a crowded of people that nobody liked. Oftentimes, when people judge us we tend to believe what they say about us, and allow it to hold us from walking in God' divine calling. It wasn't Zacchaeus' fault that he was lacking in height, but it was his fault he was lacking in spirit. He overcomes this problem by putting aside his dignity and climbed a tree. He perseveres in the face of obstacles, criticism and aims straight for Jesus, Our Lord and Savior.

A man's life does not consist in the abundance of his possessions or the accumulation of material things. It doesn't give you true happiness, satisfaction and definitely no salvation. We can learn this from Zacchaeus, our party friends, the mighty dollar bill, the pleasures of life, and accumulation of material things.

For what shall it profit a man, if he
shall gain the whole world,
and lose his own soul?
Mark 8:36 KJV

God will never reject or cast you away, just believe on the Lord Jesus Christ, and you will be saved.

If you declare with your mouth, "Jesus is Lord," and believe in your heart that God raised him from the dead, you will be saved. For it is with your heart that you believe and are justified, and it is with your mouth that you profess your with and are saved. As the Scriptures says, "Anyone who believes in him will never be put to shame. For, "Everyone who calls on the name of the Lord will be saved."
Romans 10:9-11,13 NIV

According to Clement of Alexandria, a Christian theologian, Zacchaeus was surnamed Matthias by the apostles. He took the place of Judas Iscariot after Jesus' ascension. The later Apostolic Constitutions identify "Zacchaeus the Publican" as the first bishop of Caesarea. The Beatitude, Matthew 5:8, "Blessed are the pure of heart, for they shall see God," stated by Jesus is used to illustrate the biblical story of Zacchaeus because his name means "pure." In Jericho, there is a large square tower which by tradition is named the House of Zacchaeus.

There is also a Sunday called "Zacchaeus Sunday" when the gospel account of Zacchaeus is read on the last Sunday following the preparation for the Great Lent. In Eastern Orthodox and Greek-Catholic Churches of Slavic tradition, this is read because Jesus' call to Zacchaeus to come down from the sycamore-fig tree symbolizes the divine call to humility, and Zacchaeus' repentance heart.

Side Note: According to the Gospel of the Thomas: The Childhood of Christ, Zaccheaus was also the name of the teacher of the boy Jesus. C.M. Kerr

CHAPTER 4

Jesus Entered and Passed

And Jesus entered and passed through Jericho.
Luke 19:1 KJV

Jesus was passing through Jericho on His way to Jerusalem, where the events of Holy Week would soon take place. He was on His way to Jerusalem, where He would celebrate the last supper with His disciples. Many, many, many Jews from Galilee were passing through Jericho that day on their way to observe Passover in Jerusalem.

I feel a need to briefly explain "Holy Week." May I?
smile and praise God

On the Sunday before his death, Jesus began his trip to Jerusalem, knowing that soon he would lay down his life for the sins of the world. Day 1 is Palm Sunday and Jesus' triumphal entry into Jerusalem, the crowd welcomed him by waving palm branches. Day 2, Monday, Jesus clears the temple of corrupt money changers by overturning their tables. Day 3, Jesus was back at the temple, and then later at the Mount of Olives where He gave the Olivet Discourse. Tuesday is also the date that Judas Iscariot negotiated with the Sanhedrin to betray Jesus. Day 4 is called "Silent Wednesday," because the Bible doesn't say what the Lord did. Day 5, Jesus washed his disciples feet and then shared the feast of Passover. During this Last Supper Jesus established the Communion, instructing his followers to continually remember his sacrifice by sharing in the elements of bread and wine, later they when to the Garden of Gethsemane where Jesus prayed to God the Father, and late that evening in Gethsemane Jesus was betrayed with a kiss by Judas Iscariot and arrested by the Sanhedrin. Day 6 is Good Friday, Jesus' Trial, Crucifixion, Death and Burial occurred. Day 7, Jesus body lay in the tomb, guarded by Roman soldiers. Day 8, Resurrection Sunday! On this day, Jesus Christ made at least five appearances. Jesus first appears to Mary Magdalene, also Peter, the two disciples on the road to Emmaus, and later that day to all of the disciples except Thomas, while they were gathered in a house for prayer.

In Jesus' time, Israel was not a free nation. It was under the control of the Roman Empire. They had to obey their laws, submit to their authority, and pay taxes commanded by them which support their country. Jericho was a major entrance into Roman controlled territory as well as a major tax collection site which Zacchaeus oversees working for the Roman government.

During the time of Jesus, the publicans and tax collectors could walk up to a man and tax him for what he was carrying. Every man was to pay 1% of his annual income for income tax, but other taxes were imposed, like import and export taxes, sales tax, property tax, emergency tax, crop taxes.

These taxes went to the Roman Empire to help maintains the roads, security, religious freedom, and a certain amount went to tax collectors. These tax collectors were often corrupt, and hatred by many. They were hated because they were dishonest and cheated people by collecting more money than they were supposed to. They would give Rome their assigned portion of the revenue and kept the rest for themselves.

It was actually a Roman official who was ultimately responsible to Rome for collecting the revenue of the province, but they would sell the rights to extort tax to the highest bidders, most of the time a Jewish citizen.

Tax collectors like Zacchaeus; a Jew was especially looked down upon by the Pharisees, rulers, and fellow Jews. To them, he was among the worst of sinners and viewed him as a traitor for working for the Roman Empire. Zacchaeus wouldn't have been allowed to worship in the synagogue with other Jews, but here Jesus was inviting Himself to a tax collector's house as those he was His friend.

Even though, Zacchaeus was regarded by the rest of the Jews as a deserter of one faith, unworthy to be numbered among the sons of Abraham, he was still chosen by the Lord to be His host. I would like to say that the social outcast of life is still a son of God, within whose heart the spirit of Christ is longing to make it abode "For the Son of man came to seek and to save that which was lost."

**This righteousness is given through faith
in Jesus Christ to all who believe.**

**There is no difference between
Jew and Gentile,
for all have sinned and fall short
of the glory of God,
and all are justified freely by his grace
through the redemption that
came by Christ Jesus.**
Romans 3:22-24 NIV

Now, the city called Jericho is one of the most well-known bible places in bible history. It is mentioned 59 times in the bible but only 5 fives in the New Testament. The Gospel of Luke mentions it 3 of the 5 times in the New Testament. In Luke 10:30, it states a certain man went down from Jerusalem to Jericho, and fell among thieves. Then in Luke 18, it tells us when Jesus came near to Jericho, a certain blind man sat by the way side begging, and then Luke tells us as Jesus entered and passed through Jericho that's where he met Zacchaeus, Luke 19:1.

However, the Old Testament speaks of Jericho, the most. Jericho's name in Hebrew is "Yeriho" is thought to derive from Canaanite word "Reah" which means "fragrant." Jericho's name was also thought to mean "moon" which is "Yareah" in Canaanite since the city was an early centre of worship for lunar deities. Note that, the Jericho's Arabic name, Ariha means "fragrant" and is derives from the same Canaanite word "Reah" which has the same meaning as in Hebrew.

The name Jericho means "place of fragrance." The original Jericho was a place of fragrance, a fenced city in the midst of a vast grove of palm trees in the plain of Jordan.

Jericho was the centered of the lucrative production and export of balsam. The Balsam of Mecca and also called the Balsam of Gilead is a resinous gum of the tree Commiphora gileadensis. The resin was used in medicine and perfume in ancient Greece and the Roman Empire. The plants were known for the expensive perfume that was produced from it, and well as for exceptional medicinal properties that were attributed to its sap, wood, bark, and seeds.

Jericho was located about 5 miles west of the Jordan River, 7 miles north of the Dead Sea, and approximately 800 feet below sea level. It was extremely humid with intense heat in the summer. It was known as the City of Palms because it had many date-palm trees, Deuteronomy 34:3. It was located 1 mile northwest of the modern day city of Jericho.

The first time Jericho it is mentioned is in the bible is in the book of Numbers.

**And the children of Israel set forward,
and pitched in the plains of Moab
on this side Jordan by Jericho.**
Numbers 22:1 KJV

In its day, Jericho was the most important Canaanite fortress city and the strongest in the Jordan valley. It was also directly in the path of the advancing Israelites, who had just crossed the Jordan River, Joshua 3:1-17.

The battle at Jericho is the first battle of the Israelites during their conquest of Canaan. Jericho was destroyed primarily because while under Canaanite occupation, it would have, as it does again today, hindered their control of all of the Promised Land that God had deeded to the descendant of Abraham, Isaac, and Jacob long before—Dan to Beersheba, the Jordan to the Mediterranean, every last square inch.

Jericho was taken in a very remarkable manner by the Israelites by the mighty hands of God, Joshua 6. The walls of Jericho fell after Joshua and the Israelite army marched around the city once every day for six days with the seven priests carrying ram's horn in front of the ark.

Note of Interests: The city of Jericho had two walls. The outside wall was six feet thick, and the inside wall was twelve feet thick. These walls were structured on a three tiered plan. The walls started with an earthen embankment, then an upwards stone retainer wall which stood about 15 ft. high. On top of the stone wall, stood another wall made of mud-brick, 6 ft. thick and 25 ft. high. Also, at the crest of this embankment was another similarly sized wall whose base was about 45 feet above the ground level outside the retaining wall. So if you were standing in front of the retaining wall, it would appear to be as tall as a 10 story building. The upper city within the top walls of Jericho was 6 acres, and the fortification rampart around the upper city was 3 acres, so the total area of Jericho was about 9 acres, with about a 1/2 mile circumference. The population of Jericho within the Upper City was around 1200 people. However, people were living in the space between the walls of Jericho, on the embankment, and houses were built as part of the wall, as well. When archaeologists' discovered this fact, the Bible was once again verified unintentionally by science. Rahab immediately comes to mind, Joshua 2. The book of Joshua relates how Rahab's house was built into the walls of Jericho, and the spies escaped out of the window, sliding down the walls of the city, Joshua 2:15. She then hung "cord of scarlet thread" out of her window, Joshua 2:17-21. The scarlet thread would have been plainly visible if her house were indeed built into the walls.

On the seventh day, they marched around the city of Jericho seven times and then the priests blow their ram's horns. Joshua ordered the people to shout, and the walls collapsed. The city was destroyed. The silver, gold, vessels of brass, and of iron were reserved. It was placed in the treasury of the house of Jehovah, Joshua 6:24. Rahab and her family were the only ones spared because she had hidden the two spies sent by Joshua. After this, Joshua burned the city, and a curse was declared upon anyone who rebuilt the city.

**Joshua adjured them at the time, saying,
Curse be the man before the Lord,
that riseth up and buildeth this city Jericho:
he shall lay the foundation
thereof in his firstborn,
and in his youngest son shall
he set up the gates of it."**
Joshua 6:26 KJV

The city remained in ruin for over 400 years. In the time of Ahab and Jezebel, Jericho was rebuilt, "In his days did Hiel the Bethelite build Jericho.

He laid the foundation thereof
in Abiram his firstborn,
and set up the gates thereof in
his youngest son Segub,
according to the word of the Lord,
which he spake by Joshua the son of Nun."
1 Kings 16:34 KJV

Hiel the Bethelite, first born son died soon after the foundation was laid for the rebuilding Jericho. He continued to work on the rebuilding of Jericho. The rest of his children died as he was rebuilding the city, until only his youngest son, Segub was left. Just as Hiel was in progress of finishing Jericho by set up the gates of the city, his youngest son Segub died. He found himself childless. The curse was fulfilled more than four hundred years after it was uttered.

By the time of the coming Jesus Christ, Jericho was an active city near the Jordan River. John the Baptist baptized not far from Jericho. Jesus Christ visited Jericho where He taught and healed those who had faith.

CHAPTER 5

Sycamore-fig Tree

The "Sycamore-fig Tree" symbolizes divinity, eternity, protection, and strength. It's also called fig-mulberry sycamore, or sycamore. They are a fig species that has been cultivated since ancient times. They belong to one of earth's oldest family of trees called Platanaceae. Scientists estimate that their family is over 100 million years old, and they can live as long as 600 years, and grow as high as 100 feet. They are a native to the Middle East and North Africa.

The sycamore trees have broad, coarse deciduous leaves which are shaped similar in shape to a mulberry. Their trunk and limbs are mixed green, tan, and cream. The tree bark will eventually turns to a smooth white when the tree matures.

The fig is an edible fruit about an inch long, ripening from a greenish color to yellow or red. There could be up to two crop harvest per year depending on the rainfall and temperature. They taste a little sweeter than the common fig and look very similar to the common fig but smaller. The fruit develops in the axil of leaves with one or two figs set together. They have been a major food for people of the Middle East for thousands of years. Their ability to store easily by drying them made them dependable long-term food source.

The Sycamore-fig Tree was considered the Ancient Egyptian's "Tree of Life." They cultivated them, and some of their mummies caskets were made from the wood of the Sycamore-fig Tree. Inside the Egyptian's tombs, the Sycamore's fruit, timber and even the twigs are represented.

In the Bible, the fig tree is referred to widely through the Old Testament and New Testament. It's the third tree to be mentioned in the Bible. The first is the "Tree of Life" and the second is the "Tree of the Knowledge of Good and Evil," Genesis 2:9.

The leaves of the fig tree were used to make coverings for Adam and Eve when they realized that they were naked, Genesis 3:7. The Promised Land is described as "a land with wheat and barley, vines and fig trees, pomegranates, olive oil and honey," Deuteronomy 8:8. There you will always have food and never lack anything.

Abigail took David and his army 200 cakes of pressed figs along with 200 loaves of bread, 2 skins of wines, 5 dressed sheep, 5seahs of roasted grain, 200 cakes of raisins, 1 Samuel 25:18.

During Solomon's reign over Judah and Israel from Dan to Beersheba each man lived "under his own vine and fig tree," an indicator of national peace, prosperity and wealth, 1 Kings 4:25.

During King Hezekiah reign, the Assyrian commander attempts to sway the army of Jerusalem by offering deserters their own vine and fig tree, 2 Kings 1:31-33. King Hezekiah's had a life-threatening infection which was cured by "a poultice of figs," 2 Kings 20:7.

In 1 Chronicles 27:28, King David appointed Baal-Hanan the Gederite as the overseer to take care of the olives and sycamore-fig trees of the western foothills.

In the book of Psalms, sycamore-fig trees are listed as a source of food destroyed in the plagues inflicted on the Egyptians, Psalm 78 42-48.

Proverbs 27:18 states, "Guarding a fig tree as looking after one's master."

The prophet Isaiah makes a contrast between sycamore-fig trees and cedar trees when the Lord's anger was against Israel, Isaiah 9:10.

The figs and fig tree are mentioned the most in the Book of Jeremiah compared to the other books of the Bible, Jeremiah 5:17, Jeremiah 8:13, Jeremiah 24:1-5, Jeremiah 24:8, and Jeremiah 29:17.

The sycamore-fig was mentioned in the book of Amos. The prophet Amos refers to his secondary occupation as a dresser or tender of sycamores, Amos 7:14

The prophet Amos occupied the most humble position in the society of his day. No one, but the poorest cultivated sycamore figs for it was hard labor.

**I was neither a prophet nor
the son of a prophet,
but I was a shepherd, and I also took
care of sycamore-fig trees.**
Amos 7:14 NIV

Jesus Christ made a number of references to fig trees, Matthew 7:16, Luke 21:29-31.

Jesus Christ put a curse on a fig tree that was in full leaf but had no fruit as a good productive tree should have had by that time of the season, Matthew 21:18-22.

The parable of the budding fig tree is found in Matthew 24:32-35, Mark 13:28-32, Luke 21:29-33 as part of the Olivet discourse.

Mark 11:12-20 includes an account of Jesus cursing the fig tree. A parallel is found in Matthew 21:18-22, but the fig trees withers immediately and is noticed at that time by the disciples.

The parable of the barren fig tree is a parable of Jesus recorded in the Gospel of Luke 13:6-9. A vine keeper holds out hope that a barren fig tree will bear fruit next year.

In Luke's gospel, short Zacchaeus resorted to climbing a sycamore in order to get a better view of Jesus in Jericho, Luke 19:4. Sycamore trees were planted on the sides of roads to provide shade for travelers, and some were planted along the road that Jesus took that day.

James used figs to describe appropriate Christian Living, "can a fig tree bear olives?" James 3:12

In the last book of the Bible, figs are used to symbolize a sign of the great end-time, "the sixth seal."

**The sun turned black like
sackcloth made of goat hair,
the whole moon turned blood red, and
the stars in the sky fell to earth,
as figs drop from a fig tree when
shaken by a strong wind.**
Revelation 6:12-13 NIV

NOTE OF INTERESTS: A Sycamore saves St. Pauls' Chapel

The St. Paul's Chapel was built around 1766, it is one of the oldest churches in the region, and it stands across the street from where the World Trade Center Towers once Stood. A 70 year old sycamore tree fell, when the World Trade Towers collapses on September

11, 2001. Its branches shielded the chapel from falling debris. St. Paul's Chapel later served as a base for rescue and recovery operations after September 11th. The tree itself did not survive, however, the sycamore's role as the chapel's protector has been memorialized by Pennsylvania artist Steve Tobin. Tobin cast the tree's remaining stump in bronze, and on September 11, 2005 the bronze stump was place in the courtyard.

CHAPTER 6

The Number Four

The number four represents God's creative works associated with earth. The material creation of the earth was completed on the 4th day. God placed the sun, moon and stars in the sky to give light to the earth and to govern the day and night, Genesis 1:14-19. The living creatures were created on the 5th and 6th day.

Here's a list of what God created and the day He did it on:

Day 1   The heavens, the earth, light and darkness
Day 2   Heaven
Day 3   Dry land, the seas, and vegetation
Day 4   The sun, the moon, and the stars
         <u>On the 5th and 6th day God created living creatures:</u>
Day 5   Living creatures in the water, birds in the air
Day 6   Living creatures on earth, land animals and man
Day 7   God rested

A unique and profound emphasis on the earth in found within Proverbs 30. The grave, a barren womb, the earth not filled with water, and the fire that never says enough are four things that are never satisfied, Proverbs 30:15. Four things in the earth that are to wonderful to understand are the way of the eagle in the air, the way of a serpent upon a rock, the way of a ship in the midst of the sea, and the way of a man with a maid, Proverbs 30:18. Proverbs 30:21 states, four things the earth cannot bear, "for a servant when he reigned, for a fool when he is filled with meat, for an odious woman when she is married, and for a handmaid that is heir to her mistress." Proverbs 30:24 tells us there are four things which are little upon the earth, but are exceeding wise, "the ants, the badgers, the locusts, and the spider. In verses 29-31 of Proverbs 30, there are four things that strut upon the earth, "a lion, a rooster, a male goat, and a king whose troops are with him.

Throughout the Bible, the number four demonstrate how God is involved in the affairs of man. Four women gave birth to the fathers of the 12 Tribes of Israel, (Leah, Bilhah, Zilpah & Rachel). Jesus was of the tribe of Judah. Judah was Jacob's fourth son, Genesis 29:35.

The Israel camp was divided into four parts when camping around the Tabernacle, Number 2:1-34. The four materials of the Tabernacles were silver, gold, brass and wood. The four covering of the Tabernacle were goat's hair, ram's skins, badger skins and fine linen. The four ornamentations of the curtains were three colors (blue, purple and scarlet), and one pattern (the cherubim).

The manna eaten by the Israelites for forty years has a four-fold description. It was small, white, round and taste sweet, Exodus 14:14, 31.

Leviticus 11 speaks of four unclean animals. Three of the animals chewed the cud, but did not divide the hoofs which are the camel, hare, and coney; while one divided the hoof, but did not chew the cud which is the swine.

Four rivers flowed out of Eden, (Pishon, Gihon, Tigris & Euphrates), Genesis 2:10-14.

The altar was foursquare, Exodus 27:1.

Four consonants formed God's Divine Name, YHWH.

The people of God had four divisions of the day associated with the daily liturgical sacrifice: Dawn to 9am, 9am to Noon, Noon to 3pm and 3pm to Sunset.

The outer cloaks of the Israelites were required to have four tassels at each corner with blue thread in each one, to remind them to obey the Lord's commandments, Number 15:37-41.

On Mount Carmel, Elijah had four pots of water poured on the sacrifice, 1 Kings 18:33.

Nehemiah's enemies sent for him four times, Nehemiah 6:4.

Four centuries were seemed by Job, Job 42:16.

The fullness of material blessing in the earth is described in Isaiah 60:17, "for brass I will bring gold, for iron I will bring silver, for wood I will bring brass and for stone I will bring iron."

In Ezekiel's vision of the heaven throne/chariot the cherubim each had four faces and bodies with four wheels, Ezekiel 1:10-12. The four acts of Judgment in Ezekiel 14:21 are sword, famine, evil beasts, and pestilence with which God condemns the idolaters of Jerusalem.

In the fiery furnace there were four men seen walking and "the form of the fourth was like the Son of God," Daniel 3:25.

Zechariah's prophecy has a reference of four horns that scattered Judah, Israel and Jerusalem, and four craftsmen that will come to terrify them, Zechariah 1. In chapter 6 of Zechariah, there are four chariots with horses of four colors, (red, black, white and dappled). This represents the spirits of the heavens acting for God in the midst of the four Gentile powers.

The New Testament has 4 gospel accounts of Jesus' life and ministry, each one of which emphasizes a different aspect of Jesus ministry and sacrifice:

Matthew: Jesus the Son of David and King

Mark: Jesus the Suffering Servant

Luke: Jesus the Perfect Man

John: Jesus as the Only Begotten Son of God

In the book of Matthew, chapter 13, there are four types of soil, the wayside, stony, thorns, and good soil. The "Seventy" went forth with a four-fold prohibition, they were to carry, no scrip, no shoes, salute no man by the way, Luke 10:4. The first three relates to matter, while the last one related to action.

In the book of Mark, the Lord speaks of His coming at evening, midnight, cock-crowing or in the morning, Mark 13:35.

In the book of Luke 15, four things were given to welcome the lost son, a robe, ring, shoes and a kiss. Three things were material, the robe, the ring, and the shoes and one was moral, the kiss.

Zacchaeus shows his repentance by offering to repay anyone he wrong by paying it back by four-fold, Luke 19:8.

In the book of John, Lazarus was dead four days before Jesus raised him from the dead, John 11:17.

Jesus garments were divided into four parts among the soldiers, but the cast lots for his tunic which was without seam, woven from the top in one piece, John 19:23.

When Peter went on the rooftop to pray, he had a vision of a sheet with four corners and in it were all kinds of four-footed animals of the earth, wild beasts, creeping things, and birds of the air symbolizing the gospel going to all the Gentiles, Acts 10:9-16.

Philip the evangelist had four unmarried daughters who prophesied, Act 21:9.

The body is sown and raised four ways according to 1 Corinthians 15:42-44, "in corruption, raised in incorruption," "in dishonor, raised in glory," "in weakness, raised in power," and "it is sown a natural body, it is raised a spiritual body.

The types of suffering are four-fold according to 2 Corinthians 4:8 and 9. We are "troubled, but not distressed," "perplexed, but not in despair," "persecuted, but not forsaken," and "cast down, but not destroyed."

God confirmed His message by four things which are signs, wonders, miracles, and gifts of the Holy Spirit, Hebrew 2:4.

Revelation 13:7 speaks of four things satan's authority will exercise control over concerning mankind which are every lands, tongues, families, and nations. Four heavenly creatures surround God's heavenly throne, Revelation 4:6-8. Four horsemen bring calamity on the earth, Revelation 6:1-8. Four Angels keep watch at the four corners of the earth, holding back the four winds of the world, Revelation 7:1.

**After this I saw four angels
standing on the four corners of the earth,
holding back the four winds of the earth
to prevent any wind from blowing
on the land or on the sea or on any tree.**
Revelation 7:1 NIV

Lastly, the number four can be viewed as representing completeness in our present day earthly life.

1. Four is the number of the great elements: earth, air, fire, and water

2. Four things that make up the universe: time, energy, space and matter

3. Four directions: north, south, east, and west

4. Four seasons: winter, summer, fall and spring

5. Four divisions of the day: morning, noon, evening, and midnight

6. Four principal phases of the moon: new moon, first quarter, full moon, third quarter, also called last quarter.

CHAPTER 7

Son of Man

The words "Son of Man" is a phrase used in both
the Old Testament and the New Testament. The
words "Son of Man" have diverse meanings. In some
verses it's "Son of man" with the word "man" with
a lower case "m." Also in other verses, it's "son of
man" with the words "son" and "man" with lower case
letters. It is used 192 times in the Bible, King James
Version. It appeared first in the book of Numbers and
only once.

**God is not a man, that he should lie;
neither the son of man, that he should repent:
hath he said, and shall he not do it?
Or hath he spoken, and shall
he not make it good?
Behold, I have received commandment
to bless: and he hath blessed;
and I cannot reverse it.**
Numbers 23:19-20 KJV

These words were spoken by Balaam the son of
Beor, who live at Pethor, on the banks of the Euphrates
River. Balak a Moab king sent his messengers to
Balaam. He wanted Balaam to come to the plains of

Moab, and curse the Israelites. King Balak had heard how the Israelites had conquered the Amorites. He feared them and now they had camped in the plains of Moab, east of the Jordan River at Jericho.

Once Balaam arrives there, he blesses the Israelites instead of cursing them. King Balak flew into an explosive rage against Balaam. Balaam then spoke those words to tell King Balak that he had to do what God commanded him to do.

How many times did Balaam bless the Israelites? *Answer in the back of book.*

The phrase "Son of man" appears 109 times in the Old Testament but mostly in the book of Ezekiel. God called the prophet Ezekiel "Son of man" 93 times. The first time God called Ezekiel, "Son of man" is in the 2nd chapter of the book of Ezekiel.

**And he said unto me, Son of
man, stand upon thy feet,
And I will speak unto thee.**
Ezekiel 2:1 KJV

God uses this phrase at this particular time to call Ezekiel a human being. The following scriptures denote man weakness and worth using the phrase "son of man."

**How much less man, that is a worm?
and the son of man, which is a worm?**
Job 25:6 KJV

What is man, thou art mindful of him?
and the son of man, that thou visitest him?
Psalm 8:4 KJV

Lord, what is man, that thou
takest knowledge of him!
Or the son of man, that thou
makest account of him!
Psalm 144:3 KJV

Put not your trust in princes,
nor in the son of man,
in whom there is no help.
Psalm 146:3 KJV

I, even I, am he that comforeth you:
who art thou, that thou shouldest be
afraid of a man that shall die,
and of the son of man which
shall be made as grass;
Isaiah 51:12 KJV

However, when we come to the New Testament, the expression "Son of man" has an additional meaning. The phrase "Son of man" is a Messianic title and appears 88 times in the New Testament referring to Jesus Christ, the Messiah. When Jesus used this phrase the Jews of that era were familiar with the phrase and to whom it referred. Jesus was proclaiming Himself as the Messiah.

The phrases "Son of man" and "Son of God" were both used by Jesus. Jesus did not cease being God by becoming a man. Jesus clearly claims to be God when he asked his disciples who do men say he was, Matthew 16:13-17. Simon Peter answered, and said, "Thou art the Christ, the Son of the living God."

Jesus had two natures which were divine and human in one person, Philippians 2.

Though he was God,
He did not think of equality with God
as something to cling to.
Instead, he gave up his divine privileges;
he took the humble position of a slave
and was born as a human form,
he humbled himself in obedience to God
and died a criminal's death on a cross.
Philippians 2:6-8 NLT

The expression "Son of man" and "Son of God" describes Jesus in the New Testament. He was a man and He was God. Son of man is a reference to Jesus humanity. Jesus was God in human flesh, and He had a body, a human body with flesh and bones according to Hebrew 2 and Luke 24.

Since the children have flesh and blood,
he too shared in their humanity
so that by his death he might break
the power of him who holds
the power of death—that is, the devil.
Hebrews 2:14 NIV

**Look at my hands and my feet. It is
I myself! Touch me and see;
a ghost does not have flesh and
bones, as you see I have.**
Luke 24:39 NIV

Jesus was God in human flesh according to
Matthew 9.

**So I will prove to you that
the Son of Man has the authority
on earth to forgive sins.
Then Jesus turned to the
paralyzed man and said,
"Stand up, pick up your mat, and go home!"**
Matthew 9:6 NLT

Throughout the Bible, Jesus is viewed as a man
and at other times as God. This selection of verses
has Jesus viewed as both God and man.

**God promised this Good News long ago
through his prophets in the holy Scriptures.
The Good News is about his Son.
In his earthly life he was born into
King David's family line,
and he was shown to be the Son of God when
he was raised from the dead by
the power of the Holy Spirit.
He is Jesus Christ our Lord.**
Romans 1:2-4 NLT

This passage of scripture is only sayings that Jesus had a human birth, an earthly family, and He is the Son of God. Jesus came down from heaven and took the form of a man to save mankind.

When Jesus was asked by the high priest whether He was the "Son of God," He responded, "It is as you said," Matthew 26:62-64. This verse shows us that Jesus Himself used the phrase "Son of man" to indicate His deity as the "Son of God."

The "Son of man" occurs in Matthew's gospel over 30 times, in Mark's gospel 15 times, and in Luke's gospel 25 times, and in John's gospel 12 times. It is usually from the mouth of Jesus Himself that it occurs, except once, when the bystanders ask what He means by the title, John 12:34.

The people answered him,
We have heard out of the law that Christ
abideth for ever: and how sayest thou,
The Son of man must be lifted up?
Who is this Son of man?
John 12:34 NLT

Outside the Gospel, "Son of man" occurs next in the book of Acts, in Stephen's speech to the Sanhedrin.

And said, Behold, I see the heavens opened,
and the Son of man standing
on the right hand of God.
Acts 7:56 KJV

In the book of Revelation is the last place the phrase "Son of man" occurs.

**And in the midst of the seven candlesticks
one like unto the Son of man,
clothed with a garment down to the foot,
and girt about the paps with a golden girdle.**
Revelations 1:13 KJV

**And I looked, and behold a white cloud,
and upon the cloud one sat like
unto the Son of man,
having on his head a golden crown,
and in his hand a sharp sickle.**
Revelation 14:14 KJV

In reference to Zacchaeus, the chief tax collector, the expression "Son of man" is mentioned once in Luke 19 surrounding this biblical event. Jesus was speaking to Zacchaeus. Jesus had gone to be the guest of a sinner, and the people in the crowd were muttering the fact. Nevertheless, Zacchaeus stood up and said to Jesus, the Lord that he would give half of his possession to the poor and if he had cheated anybody out of anything he would pay them back four times the amount. Then Jesus said to Zacchaeus the hated tax collector:

**"Today salvation has come to this house,
because this man, too, is a son of Abraham.
For the Son of Man came to seek
and to save the lost."**
Luke 19:9 NIV

Author's Closing Remarks . . .

Now, what will come to your mind first, when you hear, read, or meet a person name Zaccheaus?

Luke 19

Sycamore-fig Tree

Son of man

Luke, the Evangelist

The Gospel of Luke

Jesus Entered Jericho

The #4

Why not? *Write a sentence or two of what comes to your mind concerning the above words.*

_____

_____

_____

_____

_____

_____

_____

_____

_____

_____

_____

Isaiah 26:3-4 "Perfect Peace VI"

As we wrap up our Ministry with You today;

Will You Pray for the Ministry . . .

May the "LORD of Peace," Himself give you Peace at all time and in every way.

Dr. Vanessa

REFERENCES

Chapter 1

1. The Gospel of Luke—Wikipedia The Free Encyclopedia, http://en.wikipedia.org/wiki/Gospel_of_Saint_Luke

2. Parable of Jesus—Wikipedia The Free Encyclopedia, http://en.wikipedia.org/wiki/Parables_of_Jesus

Chapter 2

Holy Apostle and Evangelist Luke Serbian Orthodox Mission, http://saintlukesoc.org/saint_luke.html

Chapter 3

Zacchaeus—Wikipedia The Free Encyclopedia, http://en.wikipedia.org/wiki/Zacchaeus

Chapter 4

1. Jericho—Daily Bible Study, http://www.keyway.ca/htm2004/20040816.htm

2. Holy Week, http://christianity.about.com/od/easter/ss/Holy-Week-Timeline

Chapter 5

1. eHow—Sycamore Tree http://www.ehow.com/facts_5835785_sycamore-tree-symbolize_.html

Chapter 6

1. The Bible

Chapter 7

1. The King James, NIV and NLT Bibles

2. JTS—Jacksonville Theology Seminary (Master of Theology & Doctor of Ministry)

Chapter 1

The original authors of these books wrote in ancient Hebrew, ancient Aramaic, and ancient Greek. The unction of the Holy Spirit will not allow me to leave you hanging there . . . Bear with me a little longer . . . LOL (Lot of Love) . . . Thanks

The first human author to write down biblical information was Moses. He was commanded by God, Exodus 34:27. It states, "Write down these words, for in accordance with these words I have made a covenant with you and with Israel." Moses wrote in his native language called Hebrew. Their alphabet consisted of 22 letters, all consonants. Almost the entire Old Testament was written in Hebrew during the thousand years of its composition; except for a few chapters in the prophecies of Ezra (Ezra 4:8-Ezra 6:18, Ezra 7:7:12-26) and Daniel (Daniel 2:4-Daniel 7:28) and one verse in Jeremiah (Jeremiah 10:11) were written in a language called Aramaic.

The Aramaic is a Semitic language closely related to Hebrew. Its dialect has been in used since the 9th century BC. The Assyrians made Aramaic the common language of the Near East. In exile and under the empire, Aramaic letters replaced the old (Phoenician) script for writing Hebrew. This language because very popular in the ancient world and actually replaced other languages.

Aramaic even became the common language spoken in Israel, in Jesus' time. The presence of some Aramaic words in the New Testament, "Talitha cumi," "Maranatha," and "Golgotha" suggests that Jesus spoke a dialect of Aramaic. Aramaic words were even used by the Gospel writers in the New Testament.

The New Testament, however, was written in Greek. It was the common language of the New Testament writers. Greek was the language of Alexander's empire and so the language of the East under the Romans. Greek was the language during the years of the composition of the New Testament from 50 to 100 AD.

A matter of fact, many Jews couldn't even read Hebrew anymore, and this disturbed the Jewish leaders tremulously, and so, around 300 BC the translation of the Old Testament from Hebrew into Greek were undertaken, and it was completed around 200 BC. Gradually this Greek translation of the Old Testament, called the Septuagint was widely accepted and was even used in many synagogues.

Koine Greek is basically a simplified Greek used mainly as an unofficially second language in the Roman Empire. It was also the original language of the New Testament. [Reference from www.biblica. com/bibles/fag/11/]

Mary's Song: Luke 1:46-55

My soul glorifies the LORD
and my spirit rejoices in God my Savior,
for he has been mindful
of the humble state of his servant.
From now on all generations will call me blessed,
for the Mighty One has done great things for me—
holy is his name.
His mercy extends to those who fear him,
from generation to generation.
He has performed mighty deeds with his arm;
he has scattered those who are proud in their inmost thoughts.
He has brought down rulers from their thrones
but has lifted up the humble.
He has filled the hungry with good things
but has sent the rich away empty.
He has helped his servant Israel,
remembering to be merciful
to Abraham and his descendants forever,
just as he promised our ancestors.

(try singing it out loud)

Vanessa Rayner

Zechariah's Song: Luke 1:68-79

Praise be to the LORD, the God of Israel,
because he has come to his people and redeemed them.
He has raised up a horn of salvation for us
in the house of his servant David
(as he said through his holy prophets of long ago),
salvation from our enemies
and from the hand of all who hate us—
to show mercy to our ancestors
and to remember his holy covenant,
the oath he swore to our father Abraham:
to rescue us from the hand of our enemies,
and to enable us to serve him without fear
in holiness and righteousness before him all our days.
And you, my child, will be called a prophet of the Most High;
for you will go on before the LORD to prepare the way for him,
to give his people the knowledge of salvation
through the forgiveness of their sins,
because of the tender mercy of our God,
by which rising sun will come to us from heaven
to shine on those living in darkness
and in the shadow of death,
to guide our feet into the path of peace.

(try singing it out loud)

Feast of the Passover, Exodus 12:1-28

The Passover meal commemorates the deliverance of the children of Israel from Pharaoh as slaves in Egypt, around 1450 BC. It begins on the 15th day of the Jewish month of Nissan. It is the first of the three major festivals with historical and agricultural significance the other two are Shavu'ot and Sukkot.

The first Passover is described in Exodus chapter 12. One lamb was slain for every household, and the blood was painted on the lintels and doorposts. This was done in order that the "Angel of Death" would not slay the first-born son of the Jewish households, but only those of Pharaoh's people, whom God had warned He would judge. The children of Israel were to eat the lamb with unleavened bread and bitter herbs. The eating of unleavened bread was to continue for seven days. God ordained that the children of Israel would commemorate the Passover every year to remember their deliverance, almost 3,450 years ago.

Chapter 2

Muratorian Canon is also called the "Muratorian Fragment." The Muratorian Canon lists all the New Testament books, except Matthew, Mark, Hebrews, James, 1 & 2 Peter and 3 John. The document is called a "Fragment" because portions of the document have been torn off. It's perhaps the oldest known list of the books of the New Testament. It reveals that most of the New Testament books were already recognized and accepted in the first part of the 2nd century about 150-170 AD by the early church. The Fragment consists of 85 lines and it is important since it recognizes most of the books of the New Testament and mentions their authors.

Irenaeus was born in 130 AD in Smyrna, Turkey. He was referred to by some as Saint Irenaeus a Bishop of Lugdunum in Gaul. He was an early Church Father, and a hearer of Polycarp, who in turns was traditionally a disciple of John the Evangelist. As one of the first great Christian theologian he wrote a book called "Adversus haereses" (Against Heresies) which is a detail attack on Gnosticism which was then a serious threat to the Christian Church. He died 202 AD.

Titus Flavius Clemens, known as **Clement of Alexandria** was a Christian theologian. He was born in 150 AD to pagan Greek parents and later converted to Christianity. He was well educated and taught at the Catechetical School of Alexandra, and later opens his own school in 190 AD.

Origen or Origen Adamantius was a scholar and early Christian theologian who was born in Alexandra around 184 AD to Christian parents. In 202 his father was martyred in the outbreak of the persecution during the reign of Septimius Severus. Origen was a writer in multiple branches of theology, including textual criticism, biblical exegesis and hermeneutic, philosophical theology, preaching and spirituality.

Quintus Septimius Florens **Tertullianus** (160-225 AD) was born a pagan in Carthage. He was a prolific early Christian author from Carthage in the Roman providence of Africa. He was the first Christian author to produce an extensive corpus of Latin Christian literature.

Saint **Jerome** (347-420 AD) was a Latin Christian priest, theologian and historian who also became a Doctor of the Church. He was best known for his translation of the Bible into Latin (the Vulgate), and his commentaries on the Gospel of the Hebrews.

Eusebius (260-340 AD) also called Eusebius of Caesarea and Eusebius Pamphili was a Roman historian. He became the Bishop of Caesarea in Palestine about 314 AD. Eusebius wrote a chronological account of the development of Early Christianity from the 1st century to the 4th century. He also wrote others literatures.

Chapter 3

Matthew, also known called Levi, Mathew 9:9. His post was on the road between Damascus and the seaports of Phoenicia. Zacchaeus' headquarters was in Jericho, the center of the balsam trade.

OTHER BOOKS BY THE AUTHOR:

From the Pew to the Pulpit

Isaiah 26:3-4 "Perfect Peace"

Isaiah 26:3-4 "Perfect Peace" The Last Single Digit

Isaiah 26:3-4 "Perfect Peace III" Silver and Gold

Isaiah 26:3-4 "Perfect Peace IV" The Kingdom Number

Isaiah 26:3-4 "Perfect Peace V" 2541